Light is what we live in

M. E. Cramer

Oct./14

(sister of Paul Murray)

Light
is what we live in

M. E. Csamer

Artful Codger Press
Kingston, Ontario / 2005

Printed in Canada

LIBRARY AND ARCHIVES CANADA CATALOGUING IN PUBLICATION

Csamer, M. E. (Mary Ellen), 1948-
Light is what we live in / M.E. Csamer.
Poems.
ISBN 0-9736161-4-8
I. Title.
PS8555.S25L53 2005 C811'.54 C2005-903951-5

Artful Codger Press
10 Gordon Street, Kingston, Ontario, Canada, K7M 3R9

In memory of my mother, Mary Murray
and my aunt, Fran Coughlin.
For my daughters Jen and Mandy, who lent me wisdom.
First, last and always, for Steve.

Acknowledgements

Some of these poems have been published in: *The Amethyst Review, Canadian Woman Studies, Event, (Ex)cite, The Fiddlehead, The Nashwaak Review and Room of One's Own.* 'Time to Myself' will appear shortly in *And no one knows the blood we share,* a chapbook from the Feminist Caucus of the League of Canadian Poets.

Author's photo courtesy of F&J Woods Photography

With thanks to Elizabeth Greene, my editor, for her encouragement, generosity, and astute observations. This is a better book because of her.

Contents

1

Light is what we live in

Light is what we live in

> To say is to see again by the light of speech
> Charles Tomlinson

Mother, c.1931

Light is what we live in,
how the camera captures us
through light, this captioned
photo of a girl, circa 1931,
suspended in the amber
of an early August morning.

Light is what we live in: ninety years
of light are fading from the eyes
of this girl, gone woman,
gone dowager, gone crone.

At night, she's thirsty for the past,
asks for memory, as a child would ask for water.
I bring this picture from her dresser.
"Here I am," she says, "that's me,"
offers it as proof she still exists somewhere in time
quicksilver as the light, and light as wind
that lifts those tight, dark curls.

Mom and Mike, 1940

Father, here is mother
in rocking chair with newborn Michael.
Look how the light patterns the floor,
ghost of branch and spare leaf: Fall.

She gazes at her first born son,
as if some livid little god with bile to spare
might take him from her arms, this child
who makes a marriage real.

Behind her on the bureau
you are framed in cap and jacket,
away at war, signing up
without her knowledge: this
your first abdication.

All we know of time is measured in light
and memory is light. In these pictures
I'm not yet born, but I know this light,
the searing heat of it against the eye
that looks on innocence it wasn't meant to see,
these young-old faces, I should not know
nor grieve for.

Mike, 1944

It's the tree behind you, Michael, that's why I keep this picture,
how it stands on the crest of the hill, waiting.
Every summer on arrival, that tree would call me
and I'd dash, out through the back kitchen, slam
of the screen door, slap of sandal under foot, running
to touch its rough old trunk. Its branches
were my sentry place, from where I'd look
on farmhouse, road and lake beyond, see the long
reel of summer unroll its plot of beach
and sand dunes. Fishing. Ice cream.

But you were always there like a price to be paid
the way I grew to learn fish do feel pain.
Now you ruin the picture, sitting plumb
in the middle of the frame. How old? Not two?
Yet you control the focus, set the family
in orbit around you, draw love
like a power, a weapon.

The alchemy of first born, little prince,
that there can be more,
that a son means a name continues.

I will grow up to beat you
with girls. Twins.

The moment before the shutter closes,
mother biting down on anger, father's enigmatic grin.
Between you, we, the children, held in place.
I want to know why the little girl smiles, little
glass girl smiles and smiles, crystal eyes
shattering high notes.

I want to know whose finger's on the button,
why he hides from the future's scrutiny
and did he pose the picture by intention,
the parents as bookends, as if they need
such distance, even here.

Mom, Marg and Dody, 1967

Triumphant triplicity,
the Burlingham elder sisters.
A hierarchy is a division of angels.

At Expo '67, they're posed in sliding scale,
Margaret, the tallest, then Mary.
Dorothy on the end in sunglasses,
the kind a child might wear,
white plastic with turned-up corners.
Mother seems distanced from us here
as if, in this summer of snapshots,
she's gone further than Montreal,
travelled time as well as space.

Thirty years later, she sits in the lounge
at Hallowell Home For The Aged,
Margaret beside her and Dorothy's ghost.
Each week, we come with gifts
stuffed bears, a hand-made quilt, this photo,
framed reminder she hardly glances at.

Me, it fascinates: those interlocking smiles,
no hint of grief in any eye, these three,
guardians of the family's standing,
archangels at the tomb of secrets.
There'll be no resurrection.

The collection, undated

Old photos in an album, the black
and white of us. My brother Paul
(who sat by the window, waiting, whenever
Mom went out), has gathered them
from drawers and boxes; middle child,
in search of place, has labelled each,
dated small events,
insisting a chronology of order,
as if time were made accountable at last.

Within this frame, a story moves
from print to print: should we believe it,
given light's imperfection, that unerring need
to bend?

Picture us among ourselves, three generations
posed around too small a table.
Sunday dinner: Mother's on her long, long journey.
Father feeds the extra chicken to the dog
as if he's never known want.

There is a picture of him here
in which his face is hidden by a fingerprint,
but who could leave such impact
on this Claude Rains double,
mystery man in bandage, hat and pipe.

What happens, sir, if I unravel you?
Surely,
visibility is all a matter of perception.

Paternal grandparents: a collage

How they appear in every photo,
the air between zoned to the rhythm of their breath; how,
when standing, her head tucks so neatly against his shoulder,
and sitting, their legs cross in the same direction as if
two sets of bones share one skin.
Past the shadow where the camera's sharp focus dims
you know his hand is not on her hip but further back,
that good swell of the rump under playful fingers.

What room is there here for a boy to inhabit,
a puzzling, only child? If all birth's an accident,
his is one they dine out on.
No wonder he slips from every frame, develops
in the background, reappearing fully grown
bringing children of his own to pose
almost in his place,
the same doubt edging their smiles,
as if the thought of being loved
by this pair of Scott and Zelda irresponsibles,
is the only wish of each of them, till eldest grandson
pulls his own disappearing act
leaving the younger two to carry the weight,
a granite balloon of longing
tied to each slender wrist.

Faces ribbed with shadow
caught forever in their vulnerable smiles
waiting in a drawer, forever, or until a hand
seeking some document, reaches under
a crumpled postcard, bent with the weight
of its promise, a son telling his mother:
"the mountains are too beautiful to bear."

Reaches under and behind
a cancelled cheque, a spool of thread
pulling out these pictures almost by accident;
a quick glance, then again
because the smiles have loosed a small
sharp pain behind the ribs, so that the hand
reaches back to find a chair, slips into it
curling the feet under the body, tucked position
like a diver poised on the edge of some deep pool.

Mike and El, 1964: picture unavailable

There's a photo missing, Michael,
the one you took that day. Outside my door
you waited, picked your moment
swept in to click and leave
before I could do more
than throw my arms across my breasts.

Was I wearing tights? A bra?
My blouse was on the bed
crisp from the iron, summer white
against the black of tunic, shoes;
school blazer would be hanging in the pantry
where Mom could sponge it fresh each day.

She said that blazer gave me poise.
A kind of poise
I took downstairs to breakfast.

You slip a photo in your pocket,
allow yourself this small theft
from your parents' spare bedroom
knowing, in families, how much is taken
by each from each
and what cannot be given back.

The grandkids: an undeveloped collage

Furnish memory's house with images:
your life, mother, chronicled in photographs
from the young woman whose glossy black hair
had dulled to salt and pepper before any of us arrived
to the last picture taken, shop-worn body, tiny
in its wheeled chair, eyes staring at the camera
with the puzzled gape of a starved child.

(She looks at me, a face surfacing out of water.
I hold her hand as if I could pull her to safety.
There's no safety here. The doctor says soon.
He's been saying that for days.)

So many images: in each, your eyes
full of an unappeasable longing –
what did you want from us we couldn't give you,
each of us bent by the expectation?

(Part of me, no longer a daughter.
Only a daughter's memory.)

Yet in pictures where you share the focus
with my children, you are someone else,
someone perfectly content. Like here,
a birthday party. You're caught
mouth full of cake, an avid, older child
among the cluster, as eager as any to know:
What did she get? What is it?

(I sing to your ears songs
we sang together to my children.)

Such an unexpected gift, Dear
Queen of burdens and remorse.
For me as well.
Lifted to the light by those small hands,
they charmed the years to give us time,
And maybe, for a while, each other.

(My voice is sweet and high.
It does not break. If there is a god,
he is in my voice.)

Mother and El, 1998

The mercy of settings:
this county hospital, a private room,
the cheerful babble from the halls.
I want to add: September's
crisp blue light against the window,
but no bounty, that, for you.
Restless, until I drew the curtain.

I wanted to lift you in my arms,
carry you outside for one last touch of sun,
warm on flesh,
but you had left the light already.
Between us, variegating shade
moving down to dark.

Come into the light of memory, Mother,
do not hide behind recrimination,
what was known or could have been –
there is nothing left to be sorry for,
no time left, but to forgive.

Mary and Bill, 1998

Light is what we live in   still life
light
of memory,   3 a.m.
the dimmer turns an antiseptic white to muted grey.
I picture my parents, their moment.
Her hand, grossly swollen with the fluids
her defeated body can no longer pass,
in both his own he warms it, whispers
in her ear, endearments, sixty years of marriage
stilled in disappointment; he is, at last, again,
her lover, the only one of all of us she needs
for this
infinite
hour of going.

El's first communion, 1954

Suffer the little children, even here
posed in this old photo
beautiful in first good dresses
the little Brides of Christ
hiding scraped knees
with let-down hems.

They look straight from the box,
undamaged.
Yet some
already black with pain
stare out from eyes of crystal,
eyes that give back light, a gift declined;
eyes, as I imagine the Christ's eyes,
full of knowing
the futility of innocence.

Mirage: the last picture

Light is what we live in, mother.
Light is what remains.

In the summer, in the distance,
above a hot road where the air melts and shimmers
and light, like you, becomes itself, ever shifting, ever still.

In the last of all the pictures you are waving from that place.

2

Van Gogh's Light

One of those nights

(for Erin and Hollay)

when *your entire life just works;*
when the writer you went to hear
didn't disappoint
& wore great shoes, to boot;

and after, in the pub
for hours with your English professor
who wanted nothing from you
but your company;

holy night, night of moments
the nexus, sharp as light off crystal
this night, a winter's, yet you know
beyond the roof of a Kingston pub

Van Gogh
's stars are burning
and Woolf, still dry,
writes on in a small room.

last chance / the centre

1. last chance

The lake takes the snow in. The land
yields to it, assuming
the responsibility of definition
as lake and sky become a great bowl of empty.

Look back a moment, stay frozen:
a frosted cake, a field
without footprints, a last
chance for repose, deny the pushing buds
soon to exhale their explosion.

The birds skim the surface of the lake
like ashes blown from a fire.

They are hungry for noise, mock
your craning for stillness – they are never still.

Snow dusts the blackberry bushes, limbs
of the apple tree, the overturned
boat settles back into its reverie.

2. The centre

Rain is the centre.
Its thousand lives spark in the puddles
in the laneway. Rain is inside the buds
filling them up till they flood
into leaf, flower.

That small black snake on the lawn,
he is the sleek black form of rain
and worms are rain to quench the thirst of robins.

The sky pours out from its pewter mug.
Each blade of grass is saying the word green
over and over.
On the tin roof of the shed
rain speaks in Morse   A
OK   A OK   AOK

The birds make way for me, begrudgingly.
I think I might have to eat a worm soon.
A human, out in the rain – it's the smell, I say.
Nothing like that inside and anyway
the roof is leaking.

If it was warmer, I would take off my shoes
squelch my toes in this glorious mud.

Dare you, say the birds.

Equinox 52

The birds are busy
pulling the sun on its long string
back to us.
This morning, they have tidied
the sky of any cloud
offering blue as a colour never seen before.

Yes, it is March, yes the land is covered in snow
but the birds, as always, are our visible hope
showing us how graceful we are when we let go of despair.

There is a hierarchy among birds in trees.
Other than crows who are somehow our brothers,
they leave the top branches for us, not knowing
we have forgotten how to fly.

The sun is naming the grass blade by blade.
Green is saying its name blade by blade.
The blackberry bushes are bare, but the vines
ripen in purple-red hints of sweetness to come.

This is how Spring arrives
in small steps, a cascade of minutia.

The sun falls
into the cup of our hands held out,
touches our uplifted faces
like a parent soothing an anxious child.

One Wing

One wing on the sidewalk
the bird's body eaten or decayed;

one wing, in sunlight
feathers dappled gray & brown;

one wing curved for lift-off
as if containing still

power to rise beyond the body's end
find above, a lonely solace.

Peel this moon

squeeze and pour it
down your throat
then sing,
you silver wolf, you
thing of summer, one day insect.

A clock packed with time
weary of doling out seconds
you want to swallow summer whole,
this night, this moon rising
orgasmic orange across the water
a bridge to walk to
moon-drowned
madness,

singing, singing, singing.

Gray

Wednesday, quiet as dark
gray wool, an old sweater

across the shoulders,
a telephone but no one calling;

Wednesday morning ready
to acquiesce: a hush, a hush, a hush;

silence like a stranger on the bus
reading the same book as you;

sound gone underground to escape
onus: a renunciation of meaning;

Wednesday the colour of socks
a letter that didn't arrive.

Juice

Where does this juice go, perpetual
motion of children in a playground?

I watch from the fence and, mostly, they ignore me
though my smile's returned by one solemn stare
from the top of the slide, the instant before *down*!

They know there's something important about them
to elicit the attention of strangers, though not
what it is, not that they will grow into us

the Slow, bent with memory,
whose days no longer flow

one into the next
like a graduation of waterfalls.

Electricity of *this time only:*
do these small, running feet
generate the wind?

Van Gogh's Light

light at the window is loud as any knock.

it has travelled the grid from winter
to bring us this overload.

June morning, 5 a.m.
there is nothing to get up for yet
but birds are sweeping away
the night's shattered silence

so up, up – how light stirs
that restlessness coded in the blood.

this it the light to be sixteen in,
weightless as rapture, walking home
to parents, anxious, at the door.
for them, it is dawn, for you
the night is still livid with moon.

this is the light
of cheerful, singing drunks,
light from the surface of Venus with flashbulbs,
Van Gogh's light to blind, wipe from memory
all colour but yellow.

this is light that says the sun is coming and coming
and one day will arrive.

Summer leaves a fingerprint

a note to say round, comes round.

So you bend to the sidewalk
in the bright sun of early morning
to trace with fingertip in rough concrete
the delicate fossil of a leaf, deeply etched,
a stone autumn appearing backwards out of winter
disjointed, like you

the self who looks up quickly to share
this accidental masterpiece

the ghost shape   of leaves

out
lined   on the

broken   side
walk:

share the intake of breath, astonishment
rounding the mouth

and later,
tries to speak of it but uses the wrong words,
the thing itself mute beneath language, inexplicable

words in place of
picked through maps of the misbegotten,
directionless

a hundred small beauties coming to our eyes each day
and why one is picked to save above another,

what that says about the elemental hexagons,
cells of the essential in memory's honeycomb.

To my daughter who now teaches others as well

Along with your sister, you taught me patience,
how to see things on their own terms: the complete
world an ant hill makes, how the wind
has a sense of humour.

You taught me justice as more than a word.
When you shouted *that's not fair!* it entered me like an edict
from the great wealth that sent you, not out of its excess,
but from the core of the motherlode, saying
here is this perfect thirst.

Now the luminous faces look to you
from their kindergarten chairs and you must become
a mirror to those faces, giving back the light –
did you learn from my learning, that the teacher
is the student is the teacher is the student,
as I am learning again, distance this time,
the sight of your back going down the street,
memory of my mother watching me
and her mother, and her mother?

All that we learn is what to let go of,
what is not love, that we come,
that we come to earth with so much wanting,
our empty cups held out to each other;
that thirst contains its own quenching
as the child at birth,
in its separation from the mother,
leaves behind such emptiness,
yet such transcendent, radiant attendance.

Not so lucky for the pigs

The wind is looking at us
with its telescopic eye,
it is coming, we can't stop it,
it wants some roofs to play with,
a car or two.

Mid afternoon night
and a dreadful silence –
where do the birds go? Has someone
seen the cat? Here is the sound, like a tunnel
suddenly given voice.

John Stevens lost his barn, lucky
the pigs went to slaughter last week.
Not so lucky for the pigs. Someone said
they saw a cow overhead but that's just Chagall.

Between storms, the rebuilding. And why
not, where should we be but here?
Hiding in mountains, ready to slide down?
On coasts that may crack off from the Earth?
Our fate, we see coming for miles.

The wind is no event.
It is a collector.
Listen: there's a story in every breath.

Elevation *10.13.00*

A man lifts a small girl up in his arms
so she can reach the cord to pull the light on
because it is dusk
because her red corduroy dress is soft in his hands
and beneath it, the beat of his life, going on.

The cord of the light waits
her hand, stretching, waits
light, fading in the sky, waits
for me to turn the corner.

Little girl's fingers tingling to touch the cord,
the man's face alight, the pink
blush in the sky, the table
where the man sits, cleared, dinner
over or not yet begun.

Thirty seconds to turn, John Street to Patrick,
an instant to notice, stop
then a time that isn't counted
the red corduroy dress
the two faces, similar
under the matching black hair
a sense of someone in the house,
a woman perhaps, in the doorway
of the room, smiling
a plate in her hand or a dish towel.

Solstice

the month of strawberries
peaks
          casting its pinnacle of light
on the performance of the colour green

while the lemon morning spreads itself across the Bay

strawberries
are the pulsing heart of this month come to flower

strawberries are sex in the mouth

after today   it is already the beginning
of goodbye   the sun turning its back
dragging the cover of warmth
               to the other side of the bed

but we have strawberries and we don't care.

The DNA of Leaning Posts

It's the posture of trust that draws the eye,
an ordinary day in the park feeding squirrels
but she leans against her father with such
a casual sense of ownership; the way he's crouched,
one knee and a hand down for balance, he almost
surrounds her small body, and his pride
at being that protection sings in every pore, his face
an ad for fatherhood where the model has only
this one job and wants no other.

For years this snapshot, framed on his desk
has whispered to me coming in with polish
or a late night cup of tea, quietly telling
a tale of a day, a life, where a father and child
speak a private language, its nouns and verbs
common enough but put together piecemeal,
a patchwork language, something to do with how
she holds the thumb of his dangling hand
in her small fingers
as if it is something that belongs in her hand,
just another part of her, sometimes elsewhere
but always held when close, that pulse
she loves the rhythm of.

A picture, not especially noticed when taken, one of many
quickly flipped through to find a few to send the grandparents,
now working quietly, as if it knows the impact of that, how subtly
to take the eye, open the ear

to its message, how it thinks science
ought to make a deeper search, map the DNA
of all our cells; of longing, its fulfillment,
this father, disposed since birth
to curl his body into a small girl's leaning post.

about hummingbirds and night wind

small winged creature
moving
at the speed of desire: that much wanting
and so little flesh to hold it.

he comes at the beckoning
of flowers planted to attract his mystery
consolidation of heat & power   a heart
unleashed in air.

how would he sleep?
and yet   last night
          in the wind
somewhere   he was nesting

waiting to appear   embroider a day
from the same cloth: that wind
last night   removing all tiresome bugs

leaving only   fireflies in the grass   miniscule green storms

beside my fingers   or maybe spears
the stars threw down.

The Ache of a Small Boned Woman

The ache of a small boned woman
is that she has carried too much,
has too much to carry,
the distance of a long life, she cannot
fly though bones grow hollow.

The ache of a small boned woman
lives in the curve of spine, how the babies
pulled her out and down towards the earth,
towards this cracked drying. The generations
march out of her bones, knocking for luck.

The ache of a small boned woman
is that she is enormous and it can't be seen,
a universe, compact as a black hole,
a story in every twist of sinew, every
fissure, marrow dissolving to make room.

The ache of a small boned woman
throbs in the garden where she stands
growing forgetful, worrying the knot of sciatica,
the garden taking her in: bone meal mulch
sift of bone dust, fine human sand.

Ordinary Miracle

The snow is always falling
and every time this morning comes around
be it five, ten, twenty-three years away
I become that new mother again
on whom the world bestows its power to content:
I know the meaning of arrival.
I have seen eyes that were my eyes and not my eyes
open and look at me from faces that were my face
and not my face and I have felt such *recognition*,
such belonging, as if the world
had opened up at last and let me in.

The snow is falling, saying hush, they sleep,
you must not wake them
or else, like dreams, they disappear
for how does one believe,
how bear the weight of such joy
and how give thanks, and then, to whom
with god gone deaf and husband equally astonished
unable to take credit, beyond the act of reproduction
for these beings who have landed in his life and mine.

This was not what we expected:
yes, the fingers, toes, the small
bodies, striving red from the struggle
but not the eyes, the breath, the power
to move us beyond words
though words are born
then and now because they must be,
must help us come to terms with this bequest
this boon, this bounty, with having been
without
and then
within
then suddenly, complete.

It snows, my daughters, still
this morning and forever;
what else is pure enough
what other thing so common, so divine
could welcome you?

Night Train

Night is a dark army on the move.

Fingers press against the glass: I want
out   to prowl the hills   fly
like Mad Witch   into the night's
eventfulness.

At Cobourg   an old man
leaves the train, walks down the road
no car in sight. He seems to prefer
this wide emptiness
to daylight's mob of company.

The darkness   edged
by a line of streetlights:
under each   his face in reverie
shoulders hunched
as rain adds its weight
to the night's
overall strategy.

We pull away, retaining his loneness
as the solitary thought in this sleeping car
while   over the lake

lightening   strobes
    sh sh   sh
in rhythm with the wheels.

I cannot sleep with the huge night
mocking all sensible acts.
I ride the intimate breath
of a dozen sleeping strangers
the soft chatter
of two conductors
in their pool of light at the end of the car.

Guests of the night, we ride its sufferance,
chimerical hands laying down track
for this
unending journey.

Do I dream the station at Kingston?
The waiting husband? Or am I the dream?
Do I invent myself from lack of sleep,
the night's official observer?

What if I made up the world from hope
and a few small dreams? What if
Prometheus is still considering his options?

Then the suddenness of a freight train
we overtake hulk-
ing oil cars spectres of flat beds boxcar, boxcar
engine brute – and past

the Cyclops of its headlight beside us still
while the mind retains a vision:
engineer at his window riding

the electric night, triumphant.

Time to Myself

Maybe it isn't a new millennium. Maybe my daughters are still children and the reason they are not here at the cottage, early this June evening is because they have gone with Grandma and Uncle Paul, to town for ice cream while I have stayed behind to have a little time to myself. Maybe time is like that, malleable, and only when we lose our faith in the impossible, do we go into that room of muscled clocks, where the counters click over until death says: it's time.

I am supposed to believe that it is twenty years since those little girls went for ice cream but this is also impossible: that their Grandma is dead, their Uncle Paul, gone to sea in a bottle. Who is to say, anyway, the dust on the road is not their car coming back and Jenny will have the story about a bird hitting the side of the car, then blowing in on her lap, a story she will tell over and over, each time with less fear, more curiosity: why did the bird pick her? Oh, you and your animals, we will answer while she shakes her head impatiently, knowing the bird meant something, but having no words yet for that meaning. For the frantic motion, then stillness.

So maybe it's a bargain: let time pass in order to have these small lights turning themselves on in the mind's back room when we come in from digging in the garden or whatever the particular connective tissue we make of time, soft light of memory falling on the good and bad at once, confusing recollection so that it is all of a piece, all necessary, part of a reverie we come out of, asking: what time is it? when what we really mean is: where are we now?

But maybe not a bargain. Maybe a gift instead, one we buy ourselves: something beautiful yet flawed (the only way we could afford it) like a puzzle so large and intricate you never can finish it, never can know for sure what the picture is or if there are pieces missing, like what message the bird was bringing Jenny as it rushed towards her through air solidifying into metal.

June The Month Of Light Is Spent

June, the month of light is spent
Like pennies from an open purse.
Now the summer will reverse
And take back all the light it sent.

We took in light until we glowed.
We took in light, we mainlined it.
We took in light, and now we're fit
For nothing

            for the motherlode

Of shiny bits is fading at the core.

We are lost
to the supernova vision of light carrying the head aloft

Like a tiny piece spun off the sun.
Throughout the summer's golden run
We learn a fiery song by rote.

The Reluctant Bride

White is incomplete,
the colour of oblivion,
a tune in the head without words,
someone you pass, surprised,
because you thought them dead.

Draped in white, I walk,
beneath the scattering
of prism shattered light,
ceilings joined in prayer.

I walk to you through chips of light:
we're flashed to memory.
You wait for me,
this aisle between us now

and now between us
all that may not be.
This ritual will set our lives in stone.

Can we ever be ourselves again,
ever climb down
from atop the wedding cake?

Why speak a public love –
who needs to know?
What shall I do
with the blenders and bed linen?

I am too white for passion.
Come, love, on those pretty,
matching sheets, defile me.

Corrupt this day and make it ours again.

Six Good Moons In A Playground

1: *The Moon Of Good Sense*

Never go out without your shoes on,
never swim alone.
She said it again and again, that moon
that sad mother, busy and anxious
hiding her sorry heart where no light comes.
All her children
went out without their shoes on,
swam alone.
Swamped in the sun's tide
never came home again.

2: *The Moon of Good Manners*

No, don't look
directly at the moon, no don't
it rude, she suck
you up through long
bright straw she lay on water,
she shuck your brain 'ifen you got one;
don't you be rude, you
or she get ya, yeah, you got it coming.
She never blind you like the sun, no,
not her, not she, not
lady subtle, lady thoughtful
she got her ways: look now
you done it, done for sure
watch now you, see you,
how you unwind
to babble, cackle, crack.

3: *The Moon of Good Deportment*

Well, that was a dreadful display!
Speech should be a thing of silver and grace,
move like a bird skimming water.

Those who must undo themselves
through language
I dismiss. No part of the puzzle
of this moon's wanting:
clarity's the thing,
gift of a god
whose speech can scuttle cloud.

4: *The Moon of Good Fun*

Mascot moon
waving her pennants of light
from the bleachers: stars
fired for the game
grapple and tackle, falling
in their own dust
over the argent howls of wolves,
yip of backyard dogs,
those wannabes.

5: *The Moon of Good Solace*

Be quiet. This instant.
Sky is the one place huge enough for silence.
Why did you stay if not to hear your own breath?
The others ran when sun shook out his brushes
not you, small   brave   eyes
wide open.
No place for fretting here, this zone
of absolutes poised on the edge of a faultless ideal.
But did you stay for pink of cloud, then? Was that breathing
but the sound of wishes? Now you howl
at a black betrayal. Hush, child,
even here is comfort   your silver
mother in the hallway with her candle.

6: *The Moon of Good Narration*

Snail   by a forgotten castle
crumbling, pail
overturned half   buried
beside its shovel.   Snail
laying tracks   of pure light
immaculate movement
while in the wading pool
its bubbling fountain   off
a flock of moons comes to rest
each one paler than the last
washed out water wafers
six round concepts
in the sky's meditation.

Swings in the playground
suddenly active
moving
by light's energy
unless   it's the moon's children
loose again.

3

Little no light

The Story of Me

In the story of me, a woman wakes up in the morning and asks:
how do I write the story of me? And answers herself:
in the story of me, a woman, waking, says: I need, for once,
to hear my own voice free of the words should and must.

In the story of me, a woman's true voice wishes to sound out
like a bell made of crystal and desire, like a horn in fog;
like a beam lighting the unused path with its rubble of loss
and frustration; wants to speak up for her needs
among the needs of others, a voice made of elbows
and strong, wide feet firmly planted in their own way.

In the story of me, a woman says:
I must put me on the schedule. What are my needs?
What answers
is a rustle of paper, a small cry
like a child down a well.
What answers is hunger and not enough food
in the whole world to feed it.

In the story of me a woman says: Who am I? All that answers
is a list of tasks; the list is never finished, the tasks,
never accomplished. The day is full of them,
the day belongs to them.
The lists belong to themselves in a way the woman does not.
Her life is about making lists and crossing things off.

In the story of me, a woman hears a voice say: go,
walk in the field: it's Spring and the pollen needs a dress
to cling to; imagine bees alighting on the warm cotton;
imagine a woman like yourself, walking, the skirt of her
dress alive with the round yellow bodies of bees; imagine
her moving in a buzz of contentment, a tango of tiny claws
slowly dancing the skirt to shreds; imagine the flowers leaning
in toward her, the swathe and swarm of the following
pollen, a storm of yellow over green in the air with midges;
imagine being part of the beauty each day requires to hand
off its promise to the next. Imagine a list that starts:
become a dress for bees, be a woman wearing bees and
pollen, a woman humming with the soft industry of bees.
Imagine a list that says, honey, make honey, make honey,
make honey.

In the story of me, a woman thinks of walking in a field
in a dress covered with bees and says:
but the floor needs washing,
there's a meeting at three.
In the story of me, a woman, at a meeting
thinks of a woman walking through a field in a dress
made of bees and says to herself: why is that not me?

In the story of me a woman, lying in bed, in the morning
speaking into a tape recorder hits the off button
and lies in the silence wondering where the birds have gone
that used to wake her; a woman lies
with her own wordlessness and thinks of a list that says:
die today.

In the story of me a woman wonders how despair
grew out of frustration, wonders when the lists started
and what the lists accomplish and who she is
among these tasks, this efficient, cheerful, lost woman.

A Dialogue Between Puberty And Menopause

Wasn't once enough? Here we go again.
It's not the same. You're ending. I'm beginning.
Yes, the same. Just backwards. We're a circle.
I want originality! Loneness!
You'll outgrow that. Crave connection. Association.
I won't be you!
We'll be us.
I won't be two!
You'll be more. A Russian doll's worth.

I hate all of what you will become.
I love all of what you were.
Not were, are!
But were has we in it.

I am not you!
I am still you.
Don't overcome me. I need to arrive.
I need to return.
Don't overcome me. It's not fair.
What would you have me do, forget you?
Just be quiet.
Impossible. Age turns up the volume.

You ruined your chances. Now you want mine.
There aren't any chances. There's only what happens.
I have future. You have only past.
Ha! Then I have You.

little no light

moon has a sound: it hums
out of the vast dark lake   it pulls
the fish, silver

moon is the hope of all dull things   rock
turned mirror   under the sun's
intense scrutiny

moon is the never, never land of the soul's need
to stay forever   on the verge of some new state

moon is a nation of pale, white gods seeking
a following among the night's insomniacs and worriers

the sun's weak sister
little no light

maybe the moon was alive once
but fell into the habit of borrowing brilliance
now it spins on the sun's thumb   numb with wanting

night wind is the moon fretting   over bat welfare
tides and other timetables

while the eyes of women seek
their own lost tides
drawn to its magnetic yearning:

it has no schedule for them.

I Would Say

The companionable silence of two friends reading on a couch
with feet entangled is what I'd say if someone asked me
to describe us. I would say: sadness for what's missing
which is wearable like a sweater the wrong colour
but such a good fit. I would say: days counted
and wished away but so many more not counted
and those the ones that rushed headlong into
children growing, grown, now the family's
oral history, stories told between us evenings
while the TV reruns something and one of us
puts popcorn into the microwave, the purchase of which
Jenny said meant we had finally entered the twentieth century.

I would say driving together in so many cars with the music loud
and me singing along while you beat a tattoo on the steering
wheel; where those cars went, winter picnics on frozen lakes
then driving south through the sleet, dark, not yet afraid of
accidents; to Nova Scotia in a '68 Merc, leaked like a boat,
nearly drowned my mother; west in the green Renault, 4
cylinders but took the Rockies like an eight. And how many
summer weekends going nowhere, nowhere being where we
wanted to go, being directionless becoming a direction, the
lack of what some would call ambition but we knew was a
hunger that couldn't be satisfied because of who we were
and what we settled for or traded off for a life of patches
but such bright colours.

And what would you say? What would you say
who always leaves the words to me as if
I were made of words, words another name
for both of us together but what name
do we give the silence? I would say:
even the silence is us, the silence which contains
what we think, what we think we think, what we think
each other thinks when we look up from either end
of the couch and braid our feet a little more for the room
is cold but we're too lazy and snug to get up, light a fire
in the latest rented house that finally has a fireplace, the wood
for which we gather from the fields beside the tumble-down
cottage we bought last year because the word home
appeared in both our mouths and we liked the taste of it.

Husband, the word future is in my mouth and I never thought
I'd like it there for you and I always seemed to be about
the past or at best a scramble to keep up with the present,
but here it is and if you'll bring your warm wet mouth to mine,
I'll share it.

A Child Hides

(for L)

behind the seventh rib or curled for sleep
in the ear's warm canal or under
the half moon of the thumb;
in dreams, in the chaos of wanting.

Heart's waif, this awaited one:
mysterious intangible, all elusive
wanderings that end with a face
looking in at a window
gone, as you turn at the sound of a footstep.

A child, that perfect self,
forming and reforming
as you reach, unmasked, unpretending,
to ask it come, lay its life beside yours
like a gift, like hope,
like crumbs on a path leading home
the home created for a child that was to be,
then wasn't.

Gift and loss at once, this child
refusing to be known
by the lines forming the mouth, line of chin,
cheekbone, a shade of hair, straw coloured or dark,
the small hand with its absolute identity of whorls
waving from a distance beyond calculation
that seemed, only yesterday, so close;
the hand yours is reaching for, stretched out,
a tethered bird,
the ache in the arm as familiar now as your own heart
beating its want like a drum.

The small hand slips away
as any child might loosen from you
become lost in the crowd
drawn by some bright object in that instant
when your thoughts are elsewhere
that moment between breaths
when the knot of parenthood
suddenly unravels.

This Poem

is not the great poem needed by the world now,
the poem to solve us and heal us and call us
and move us but it wants to be. Let it be the first
part of the first stroke of the first letter: let it offer
one thought to the massed human response, one
cell of our joint vocal cords crying no. Let it ask
how the mind can frame the evil the heart wishes.
Let it remember Hiroshima and let those gentle
innocent ashes fall here now and mingle. Because

Hatred caused this. Politics caused this. Pragmatism
caused this. Revenge caused this. The logic of numbers
caused this. Fear caused this. Not listening to our hope
caused this. Having to win caused this. Having too few
at the table caused this. Not asking our children
what they need caused this.

Let me ask the great poem to use me as one of its voice
steps moving up and up through the smoke to the clear
voice of tomorrow. Let me hope, against experience,
that the world is ready to embrace poetry, to martial
its creative forces against the enemies fear and greed.
Let me accept without judgement all the different ways
the people of the world need to be right, the beliefs
they need to house themselves against their fear.
Let me be one of those who go out to the wolf, put up
our hands to stop his breath so the houses
will stand until we abandon them, together.

And I will file the picture of the towers crumbling
in the album labelled *this was my time within the world,*
paste it beside a small baby in yellow socks, a man
before a tank in a Chinese square, a daisy
in the muzzle of a soldier's gun. I want to swim
in the river of all sorrow, the river too fierce for anger,
the river where no hands will be cleaned of blood until
all hands are, the river where a man named Moses
found in the bushes, brought us the mantra *thou*
shalt not kill. Let this poem be a plank in the boat
we must build to carry our human family to the world
washed clean in the flood of our tears. Let this poem
be an us and not a them. Let it refuse the word 'them'.
Let us be alone in the world without a god, or let our gods
be not better than us but only sadder.

This poem is not finished but it wants to end now.
With its hands open. This poem has flung itself
from the trapeze and hopes that hands are coming
to meet it in the dark, where voices will be singing
from the stripped clean throats of our longing.
The poem is flying towards the future to live or die
and it is free, it is free.

September's Light

Like a candle stubbed but glowing,
September's light shows
lamps on in the Millers' cottage.
First time this year, a few days
plucked from too busy a summer,
goodbye without hardly hello.

But we are made for this,
the sadness of snatched time,
not for June's eternal hope, the day's
kissy-face sun handing off to a happy
ever after moon.

We want light like us, light
exhausted, light able to carry
only the small possibilities we still believe in:
a day without rain, one red maple
in a string of rusting poplars;
that some part of us might go on
if only in memory, as light remains in memory
through the dark winter night.

The gladiator light of June
is candle power. Takes candle light
to see that duck skimming
the pewter surface of the lake.

The crickets know this,
their seethe, September's song.

insomniac on ice

sleep is a gift exchange & me with an empty box
I want sleep   gimme, gimme

there are too many thoughts
          at the night's audition   all of them bad actors

I want   to slip under the surface   of this clear
night water   but it turns solid beneath me

insomniac on ice   skating figure eights until morning

tonight
tomorrow night:
          where is the innocence of letting go?

I want to know the plot of this
          woman restless in the dark

why does the morning think it has to be so long in coming
as if it would then   be more welcome

is there a password I have forgotten?
the owl's wakefulness stares from my eyes   gone yellow

morning, a train
night has derailed from

feathers on the track.

Hot

She is waiting for the end
of another beginning, woman,
always changing:
now the heat is in the core.

She is saying goodbye
to the moon's pull, rhythm of tides;
letting go of consequence, tomorrow.
The calendar abandons its dialectic.
Memory constitutes a history.

She is cleaned out of hormones,
and will not replace them
because the letting go is part of the story.
If her bones thin, she will become a bird, take flight,
hollow bones, made part of the story.

Her unborn speak to her in dreams
whispering their would-have-been lives.
Possibilities dress in white:
the gossamer of last chance.
She walks in a desert of red sand
seeking water or blood. There is a train coming
& she will be on it, meeting herself.

A queen, crowned with the accomplishment of endings,
she is alive in the echoes of what is not alive
while every day loops on to the next.
The men she knows are running away from their lives
but her man stays, listens to her sizzle.
They are growing old, growing into themselves.
At last, a destination.

The intimate conversation with the past
happens after the children, in their other cities,
have hung up the phone. History
is in the woof & tweet of their days,
a music of remembrance.

Spring unfurls in the birdsong morning.
She stays in bed, remembering her seasons.
The fields lie cut, fallow.

Our Daughters Have Left on the Night Train

Over your shoulder the stars are bright reminders
of how much space there is between things,
these lives
that passed through our hands like water.

Husband,
I once thought I did not love you enough
because you were not in my dreams
but now I know you are all the things
that are not dreams
the here and now, the shared pain
of this loneliness as the train disappears in the distance
taking them home, where home is suddenly someplace else.

Perhaps a child is a dream
of who we might have been.

Husband, look at us,
we're patients let out after a long illness
the hectic jumble of the ward exchanged
for rooms recently cleaned, a note on the fridge
to say the milk is fresh.

October

wake to the desert of what is this day for.
that sand is a long walk.
hot sun above the planet wheel
93 billion miles away:
someone has counted
as if science was an answer.

the wash of darkness the end of day
puts out the light puts on the light
we are not afraid we are only empty.

every day, a list of tasks scored through
as if completion could be rounded up.
yesterday I saw a torn rainbow
my father called it   sundog
a new word at mid-life.   think: the sun has pets.

how small, how quickly gone, a life.
this, our most human season.
the only permanence is wanting.

but there are meadows, fields
full of goldenrod and purple aster
that will wither and stand up, ghosts
under the snow.

blue sky and a scarf against the wind, walking.

Random Thoughts Seeking Form

1.

Meno doesn't pause. It stops.
Instead there's a man in baggy pants
and slippers walking away from the door.
The black anvil of morning
rings with the hammer of day.
How does one get from the present
into the possible?
On the bare walls of the mind,
someone drawing a conclusion.
The ghosts have her, a psychic take-over.
She is not hungry, she is only starving.
Burned out with overstatement –
the rest cure of silence.

2.

Do not believe what you've been taught –
meno doesn't pause, it stops.
The black anvil of morning rings with the hammer of day.

And you were born one morning, with someone
drawing a conclusion on the bare walls of the mind.
Meno doesn't pause. It stops.

You expected guests, cotillions of praise, instead there's a man
in baggy pants and slippers walking away from the door
as the black anvil of morning rings with the hammer of day.

When now's the wrong map, the roads to when are closed –
how does one get from the present into the possible?
Meno doesn't pause – it stops.

She wanted to live
but the ghosts have her, a psychic takeover.
The black anvil of morning rings with the hammer of day.

A blank night:
overdrawn at the dream bank.
Meno doesn't pause, it stops.

The burn out of overstatement
brings the rest cure of silence
in the black anviled morning of the hammer rung day.

She is not hungry, she is only starving.
Meno doesn't pause. It stops.
The black anvil of morning rings with the hammer of day.

Blank

The heat of need sears off
doubt's outer layer
Pod opens,
flings from its centre
to rest in the soil of this day's effort
its bits and hard round chunks.

You, you there!
Give me occupation!
A brainstorm! A head, jam packed
hag ridden by words.
I want panic
the drunk's thirst,
a rapid heartbeat
fingers flying at the mind's manic dictation.

Oh, take this vapid (m)useless mind
that boils language
till it's insipid as watery peas.

Dull, dull, dull.

Well. Not my day to be given tongue, it seems.
Beast of language is hot for a rival.
Prometheus takes fire to a different island.

Blank at the window again, I watch
crows gather on leaf-less branches
in ragged conspiracies as the wind shifts west.
Here crow, take this heart for carrion.

november

light has gone and reason with it
something wrapped around my bones
squeezing the marrow to treacle:
call it hangman's rope

if I were a snake I would shed myself
oh, to be skinless
red pulp moving towards event

there is a brain and it ticks
keeping time to an old song
sing it with me

la de da de   oh oh oh

stronger voices shout us down
in the parliament of reason
the tune will not carry
I am as tired as I am angry
there is nowhere to sleep there is no one to blame

in the sky, that blue orb
calling itself moon
was once my round centre
stone
I cast
into night's wishing pool
but it skipped and would not sink and ricocheted
off the broken edge of the world
climbing the sky's ladder with sly, determined steps

Theoretical Physics

In the end there is only the agony of a man dying
though before that, there is 16-millimetre film,
a tourist whose camera will spawn a debate,
grandfather the camcorder, disaster's darling.
There is a woman in a pill box hat climbing
onto the back of a car
to recover something her husband has lost
and Theoretical Physics to prove that the loss occurred
when a bullet took a U-turn
ended up, pristine, on a stretcher.

Pages of a speech, half-finished,
will flutter in the air above Dallas
while a lunch goes cold, the invited guests
waiting and waiting. They have no radio.
The maids do and are crying.

Later, a fat man with cancer will clean his gun.
This will happen some time after the call
for Walter Cronkite
to come in early because one or two
or three or a thousand
assassins have scuttled to cover.

On November twenty-third there will be a birthday party
for my best friend's future husband who is ten years old.
I will take a math exam and fail.
I will take down all his pictures from my walls
but leave up the Beatles for no one would shoot the Beatles.

Before this, I will watch Lyndon Johnson sworn in
with Jackie beside him in her stained pink suit
which is either shock or calculation.
Now I know what they mean by
the king is dead long live the king.

The man himself, his death, is lost,
swept up in history's cyclone
with the debris of a million surmises.

How to make a space

(for Mom and Fran)

I don't know if he died
the man in the car ahead of us
(coming home from your funeral Sunday)
who was launched from the highway into air,
when his car clipped the vehicle ahead,
as he tried to get somewhere too fast, and did.

Only a week ago, I watched you struggle to sit up
out of your death a little while longer
for those of us who hadn't said goodbye.
I held your son, my cousin,
knowing already, the path to the graveyard.
Useless knowledge, lately gained.

*

I sit in my mother's chair.
It holds her imprint.
We are both sitting here.
Only time separates us.

*

We come together at your funeral, Fran,
trading stories of your courage and wit,
how you called your post-mastectomy self
utility grade chicken:
"Missing a wing or a breast."

We make a space for you beside the others,
the dead within, that choir seeking voice;
and Fran – each one's a soloist, sings out
in sharper, higher notes, their complicated
arias of what they've left unsaid.

*

I dreamed of you last night, Mother,
by the light of flame on water.
I was in an old house, found an letter
addressed to you.

I would send it on.

Blown Glass

In February's window
Winter puts her wares on view:
silver birch are blown
glass replicas of themselves
displayed against a cloth of sky
and juniper, its berry magnified in ice,
would make a ring for royalty.
On every bush and tree
the wind conducts a symphony of high notes.

What, in us, does winter call from heat?
Impossible landscape, the unutterable
beauty of this moment before thaw.
Nothing here that I can touch without melting,
        even
                my breath
threatens.

What, in us, cannot accept
this lunar landscape
shines without our sun of interest?
Science says we're nothing but a blip
in Earth's cold history,
our habitation, a futile season of pretence
before the world returns to ice,
the jeweller's glass doors
baring us at closing time.

The Name of a Flower

1.

We were clustered under the bridge
in our Saturday morning clubhouse
(leaf roof, squirrels for sentries)
with blankets, apples, the meeting
just coming to order when he appeared,
greasy black coat, straggles of hair.
Stares. Silence. Something in the gut running
because the legs couldn't. Him all seethe and noiselessness
and the hands and what they held. The eyes blank,
as if he wasn't there. *But he was there.*

It's that, in one moment, with one action
he took away what had been ours,
No explanation, no application. Just came
and took it away as if his need was greater.
We told no one. Never spoke of it among ourselves.
Abandoned our place as if a committee had been struck
to dissolve association.

*

How do I move in the world as if it belongs to me?
I almost said, move into, because I'm still on the edge
but I don't know what edge, and what the shape is –
a flat earth? saw blade teeth? He came and took away
what was ours. Peripheral, marginal man
but he took possession and neither he
nor we questioned his right.

Something in the gut running
because the legs couldn't.

2.

The city fights for space, for air.
A deadly virus turns away the casual
to other destinations. Desperate, tourism calls
the homebound out
with cheap gas, concerts:
"come together, breathe the air."

Rather say: take back the air
as other times we take back the streets
with late night walks of women, children
fearless men.

It's that, in one moment, with one action
SARS took away what had been ours.
No explanation, no application. Just came
and took it away as if its need was greater.

Something in the gut running
because the legs couldn't.

3.

On Pikes Peak, Edwin James discovered what would later become Colorado's state flower. *Cassie Bern*. On Arbor Day 1891, students voted for that state flower. *Corey DePooter*. Out of 22,316 votes, Rocky Mountain Columbine received 14,472. *Kelly Fleming*. Second place went to the Cactus, with 1,027 votes. *Matthew Ketcher*. Yet in 1899, the Women's Club of Cripple Creek discovered *Daniel Mauser* that the Columbine had never been legally adopted. The legislature corrected that mistake *Daniel Dohrbough* and in 1925, made it the duty *Rachel Scott* of all citizens to protect this rare species *John Tomlin* from needless destruction or waste.

In 1964, there was an attempt to replace *Isaiah Shoeis* the Columbine with the Carnation but the Daughters of Colorado *Lauren Townsend* rallied behind the Columbine asking: “What about the state song *Kyle Velasquez* ‘Where the Columbine Grows’?” *David Saunders, teacher.*

How do we move in the world as if it belongs to us?
Move from the border where they left us without money
or papers, not be frame but picture, know no limits,
be edgeless, never marginal but crucial?

It’s that, in one moment, the core is gone
skeleton sucked out the mouth; one moment,
one action – clubhouse, air
the name of a flower.

Spectre of the self, that’s all,
something left to carry on
Hiroshima grandfather outlined on a wall
silhouette only

but he was there.

4.

From the *Columbine Remembered* website:

“Kelly Fleming was writing her life story
on her home computer. She started it
at the very beginning, when her mother’s
water broke and she came into the world.
She had gotten to age 5.”

Walking in White

This place, home
that was yours, my mother
will be yours, my daughters;

this woman coming
from the garage, arms full of wood
remembers you, awaits you
this woman, memory dazed,
tomorrow driven, this woman, this
link in the girl chain.

this woman, this restless woman
searching the blank, white earth for clues
as if, as if

everything
            connected
                        gathered
                                    swept up
                                                made new

restless woman
conversing with ghosts or the dog
three fields over, anything
to give words to, anything, the air
full of words (no such thing
as a silent woman)

woman walking in white
casts a black shadow, so there.
woman, wind's song at her ear

caretaker over the sleeping world,
woman walking
restless woman in a time of rest:
everything tucked in, asleep
even the sun wan and lazy

out of my eyes, you look, mother
and remember, astonishing sleep
of the creatures, the land
as out of your eyes, mother, I see
this season: flag of a single leaf
semaphoring from a black bough
out of your ears, through the silence,
hear
the hiss the stars make, burning.

Sullivan's Pond

Country of my childhood, I remember
Paul and I those sun-bright winter mornings
skates in hand, trudging to Sullivan's Pond.
Little girl with older, long-legged brother
grumbling at her company. I raced the cold
to keep up. February: we breathed out ice

climbing drifts, then the sheen of ice,
faces crimson in polar wind. I remember
how the pond shimmered in the field, cold
and curved, the arc of morning,
brown and rough the fingers of my brother
lacing his sister's skates on Sullivan's Pond.

When school let out, a different place, buck pond,
where girls could only cheer the play on ice.
Young Richards and Keons, our brothers,
dreaming. We had no dreams then, I remember:
useful girls, compliant; ignorant of mornings
yet to come. Our rage gestated in the cold.

Seeds of memory: we harvest now the cold
heart of growing up, apart. Still, that pond
unites us, pool of longing. This winter morning,
touch my love beneath the ice.
I've learned that to forgive, I must remember.
Paul, my lovely, long-legged brother:

of all the family, you I keep, one brother
against the pain, each frightened cold
denial (there were many, I remember).
You knew my secret battering – that pond
no harder than my heart was growing. What ice
is this between us? When you ask how morning

ever brought renewal, this winter morning
darkens. In the gloom, I watch you, brother,
hunger for the light, while cataracts of ice
etch ever deeper in your eyes. My hands grow cold.
Our hearts could use a workout. Sullivan's Pond
is waiting still across the hills. Remember?

My longest love, remember, our totem of morning,
Sullivan's Pond. Come, long-legged, lovely brother:
Open cold eyes, yield to the heart's flame, your ice.

This motherless child

Before she was dead,
in the time we were going back and forth
Picton, Toronto, Picton, Toronto –
hope, no hope, hope, no hope.

For a break from the waiting (a blessing, a knife)
we walked the streets of Picton
late summer afternoons, through chestnut shade
by century houses whose blinded windows shadowed
the ghosts of old ladies walking their pasts. I walked
her childhood, her passing, her past.

Then hours, by her bed for hours, oddly content,
needlework for the hands, a rhythm of making,
(death busy unmaking) in stasis, time between time,
the delicate stitches – over and under and over and bright
yellow floss by the window, blue window, draws golden
with evening, come the nurses to turn her, so small
in the whiteness of sheets.

Wait. Wait and I'll weave us a blanket,
a blanket of colours, a crazy quilt of all that we were
and are and never could express and bled into silence
through which she is moving away, away. Wait.

Here is the phone and a dozen quarters, a list of numbers.
"Hi, it's me." It's me, it's me, and you all know
my voice, were all lifting receivers, all punching
my number. What is this silence we cover and cover,
all running for cover. What is this silence?

I am calling, at last, I am calling. No excuses, no waiting.
Got to hear every voice ever said it loved me; call
without apology at four a.m., five. "Sorry, I'm sorry,
the birthday, her growing, the letters, your dying."
As if forgiveness was hard, to give or receive;
we thought it was so we waited. We waited
till the very end, then the very end released us.

I was giving and asking and she couldn't speak
but her presence was a kind of forgiveness,
how the stroke didn't take her off at once, how she lasted
(not lingered, lasted), that we had those days with me
by the window, talking or singing, telling her the weather, the news,
while my hands at their work moved the way women's hands
are always moving, hers reaching up, up as if out of water, as if
for something only she can see or needs to grasp and no one
can help her not me, not even me, not even
her daughter, this motherless child.

Posed by Roses

In the family album, this small portrait
(so old and cracked, it's kept in plastic)
of you, Aunt Fran, in First Communion
dress and veil.

It is impossible to look at you for long.
You are too open; a face, bone hollow,
bird fragile,
the eyes, pre-flight,
staring from the frame.

In all this retrospective,
these faces held, fossils in amber,
there's none so fitted for the light as you;
skin like milk, pure, from the pitcher.
I want to pour you on strawberries.

Polar in your innocence, posed by roses,
that are forever on the cusp of opening,
like you, so luminous and grave,
your almost-smile, an aperture to time itself.

These words for a girl in her instant of pure light.

The typeface used in this book is
ITC New Baskerville, with
Shelley Allegro Script for display.
Design and layout by
Laurie Lewis
at the Artful Codger Press
in Kingston, Ontario
2005

Light is what we live in